Original title:
The Sapling's Secret

Copyright © 2025 Creative Arts Management OÜ
All rights reserved.

Author: Levi Montgomery
ISBN HARDBACK: 978-1-80567-444-3
ISBN PAPERBACK: 978-1-80567-743-7

In the Shade of Tomorrow

Beneath the boughs, a squirrel prances,
In shadows deep, it takes its chances.
With acorns stacked, a treasure stored,
It claims the crown, the forest's lord.

Sunlight gleams on leafy hair,
The critter dances without a care.
Whispers shared among the trees,
Of pranks and jokes in the gentle breeze.

The Veil of Life

A worm debates if it should crawl,
Or stick around, just take the fall.
With every squirm, it makes a plan,
To be the fastest in the land.

The ladybug laughs, painting her spots,
"Just take it slow, you connect the dots!"
In this garden of jokes and fun,
Life's a race but no need to run.

Hidden Paths to Light

A little mouse with cheese galore,
Squeaks of dreams and treasures more.
In secret paths, it starts to twirl,
Seeking snacks in a wavy whirl.

Near the roots, magic lies,
Where mushrooms wear their funny ties.
"Why so serious?" a toad chimes in,
"Life's a joke, let's start to grin!"

A Journey Beneath

Underground, where the gophers sift,
Moles are shouting, "What a gift!"
With tiny hats and grand delight,
They host a party every night.

With pranks and pies, oh what a blast,
They rumble, tumble, and hold fast.
In their world, the laughter's loud,
"Who's the silliest?" they sing in crowd.

Mysteries of the Green World

In the garden, whispers play,
Leaves are giggling, come what may.
Roots are plotting, deep below,
A dance of seeds, a show of growth.

Frogs in suits, they leap and bound,
To the rhythm of the underground.
Worms in hats, so dapper and neat,
Grooving on soft, muddy beat.

Rabbits gossip 'neath the moon,
Discussing carrots, a tasty boon.
While squirrels drop acorns with flair,
Yelling, "Look! I just planted a chair!"

Nature's jesters, wild and free,
Plotting pranks on a bumblebee.
In this green realm, laughter grows,
Where every root and stem just knows.

The Minuet of New Life

Tiny sprouts with a jig and a twirl,
Dance in the breeze, oh what a whirl!
Buds peek out with a wink and a grin,
Declaring boldly, "Let the fun begin!"

The sunlit leaves chuckle and sway,
Tickling the air in a merry display.
Flowers gossip, "Who wore it best?"
In the garden, they jest without rest.

A caterpillar dons a top hat,
Preparing for the ball, imagine that!
While ants march in a synchronized line,
Planning a banquet, all things divine.

Watch the raindrops, they giggle and splash,
Turning the soil into a joyous mash.
In this minuet, life leaps and bounds,
A hilarious ballet of nature abounds!

Hidden Stories of the Forest Floor

Beneath the leaves where critters scurry,
Tiny tales unfold in a frantic hurry.
A worm with dreams of being a star,
Misses his goal and gets stuck in a jar.

A squirrel with a penchant for nuts so bold,
Tries to find treasure, but finds dirt instead told.
With each little giggle shared on the way,
The forest whispers fun, every single day.

A Bud's Softest Wish

A tiny bud dreams of stretching high,
Wishing for wings so it can fly.
With a laugh, it sighs, "I'll bounce like a ball,"
But ends up just swaying, not flying at all.

The raindrops tease as they tumble down,
Splashing the bud; it's wearing a crown.
It chuckles, 'Why not, I'll dance in the breeze?'
Looks quite silly, but oh, how it sees!

Shadows of a New Beginning

In the cool shade where shadows play,
A seedling giggles, dreaming away.
It stumbled on roots that tangled its shoes,
Now trips through the forest, has nothing to lose.

The mushrooms chuckle, in colors so bright,
As the sapling fumbles in pure delight.
It twirls in the wind, then lands in a pile,
Of leaves and laughter, with its charming style.

The Silent Promise of Growth

In whispers of soil, the tiny shoots vow,
To drink up the sun and take a big bow.
With roots in a tangle and leaves all a-flutter,
They plan their ascent, shared giggles and clutter.

A ladybug lands on a fragile tip,
It shouts, "We're destined for quite the trip!"
With laughter and joy, they stretch toward the light,
Promising stories filled with sheer delight.

Guardians of the Green

In the garden, gnomes at play,
Hiding secrets in the clay.
Whispers of a leafy dream,
Stand guard with their quirky gleam.

Squirrels plot with nuts to spare,
Rabbits hop without a care.
The daisies giggle in the sun,
While ants march in lines for fun.

Each bug boasts of tales untold,
Their tiny worlds, a sight to behold.
While clouds above share silly views,
Krickets chirp their laugh-out-loud blues.

So here beneath the sky so wide,
Nature holds its funny side.
With every branch and bow they bend,
Life's a joke, and friends don't end.

The Unfolding Story

A tiny bud begins to spin,
A tale of green from deep within.
With leaves that wave and branches sway,
It reads its lines in bright display.

The sun, a critic from above,
Dances down with hearts of love.
Each raindrop laughs, a playful tease,
As roots weave stories with the breeze.

Beetles boast of daring flights,
While worms write poems full of bites.
The soil laughs with every turn,
While growth unfolds, all born to learn.

So come and sit beneath the shade,
Of every laugh that nature made.
In every sprout, there's joy to see,
A tale of life, wild and free.

Voices in the Breeze

In the park, a breeze takes flight,
Chirping birds provide delight.
Leaves are chuckling in the sun,
Making whispers, just for fun.

Trees stand tall and start to dance,
Inviting all to join the chance.
With shadows playing tag around,
The laughter echoes all around.

Bunnies hop with silly flair,
While butterflies swirl in midair.
The flowers sway, they know the tune,
With giggles bright as afternoon.

So let the winds carry cheer,
With every rustle, lend an ear.
For life's a jest in shades of green,
And joy is found where laughs are seen.

Where Life Begins

Nestled deep in earth's embrace,
Little sprouts await their place.
With a giggle, they burst free,
Reaching up to greet the glee.

Sunlight tickles every toe,
Drawing up the strength to grow.
Wiggly roots play hide and seek,
In a quest for the best peak.

The wind, a friend that loves to tease,
Twirls the leaves with subtle ease.
Each petal winks, a naughty glance,
Inviting all to join the dance.

From a tiny seed, a dream takes flight,
Filling days with pure delight.
In every bud, a joke can spring,
Such is the joy when life's in swing.

Nature's Hidden Promise

In the garden, a seed did chuckle,
It wiggled and jiggled, avoiding the muckle.
"I'll grow tall and proud, with a crown of green,
But only if birds don't think I'm a bean!"

A worm wiggled by with a grin so wide,
"You'll be a big deal, come stand by my side!"
The flower nearby burst into giggles,
"Just don't forget us when your branch jiggles!"

Echoes in the Soil

Roots whisper tales in the murky dark,
Of dancing ants and a mischief-making lark.
"Did you hear the one about the leaf who fell?
It landed on a snail and rang its bell!"

The soil chuckled, with grains that nodded,
"We're the keepers of secrets, but aren't quite prowled.
Dig deeper, my friend, and find out the truth,
You'll discover giggles, not just uncooth!"

Secrets Held in Bark

Bark holds the laughter of trees so grand,
Each ring is a giggle, each notch a stand.
"Can you hear that acorn? It's telling a joke!
It says, 'I once dreamed of being a bloke!'"

A squirrel raised an eyebrow, intrigued and keen,
"Did you know I'm the king of this leafy scene?
But let's keep it quiet, don't spoil my game,
Or I'll have to change my name to 'Silly Squirrel's Fame!'"

The Promise of Tomorrow

A tiny sprout looked out, hopeful and spry,
"Tomorrow, I swear, I'll be reaching the sky!"
But the clouds just chuckled, swaying in blue,
"We've got plans, little buddy, just wait for your cue!"

The sun winked down, with rays full of cheer,
"Keep stretching your leaves, I'll always be near!
And when you grow tall, we'll dance every day,
With shadows and giggles, come out and play!"

The Heart of the Wood

In the wood where trees do dance,
A squirrel plots his bold romance.
With acorn hats and leafy tights,
He twirls among the summer lights.

A beetle boasts of strength and might,
While crickets chirp through day and night.
They argue over who's more grand,
In merry jest, they take a stand.

The owl rolls eyes in wise delight,
As friends engage in playful plight.
Each branch and bough, a stage so fine,
For creatures bold, their jokes divine.

And if you listen close, you'll hear,
The laughter of the woodlands near.
In every rustle, chirp, and tease,
Nature's joy dances in the breeze.

Gentle Whispers of Nature

The wind confides in buzzing bees,
"Let's have a picnic by the trees!"
The flowers giggle, dressed in hues,
They've made a cake—delightful views!

The ants parade, all in a line,
In search of crumbs, they think they dine.
Their tiny chef, he waves a spat,
Says, "More for me, oh where's my hat?"

The butterfly flits, quite unbothered,
"Why do we rush?" she seems to ponder.
While rabbits hop in crazy loops,
The world's a stage for all the troops!

So join the fun beneath the sky,
Nature's whimsy always nearby.
In every sound, a jest appears,
Laughter echoed through the years.

Alchemy of Roots

A gopher dreams of gold below,
While digging through the dirt and snow.
"I'll find the stash!" he tells the crew,
But finds a sock—oh, what a view!

The mushrooms giggle, round and spry,
As critters pass with cautious eye.
"Don't trust that guy," they slyly plead,
For who knows what he'll really feed?

The tree roots gossip through the ground,
Sharing secrets, sounds abound.
"Did you hear what the brook did say?
It splashed on rocks and danced away!"

In muddy laughter, joy takes flight,
As nature's crew ignites the night.
With sneaky smiles and mischief rife,
Each tale brings magic to their life.

The First Green

The sprouts awake from winter's grasp,
With tiny leaves against the clasp.
They look around, start to debate,
"Who's the tallest? Let's not wait!"

A radish yells, "I've got the flair!"
A carrot shouts, "Now, that's not fair!"
And as the chatter starts to rise,
The gardener sighs, "Oh, my, what lies!"

The daffodils were just in bloom,
Hoping there's enough room.
"A dance-off soon!" they cheer and sway,
To brighten up the dreary day.

So here's to greens, both tall and stout,
Who always seem to know what's out.
With laughter sprouting all around,
The first green holds a joyful sound.

Fragments of Flora

A tiny seed in muddy shoes,
Dreams of growing, but fears to lose.
Wiggling worms just laugh and tease,
'You'll need a hat, or maybe freeze!'

Pigeons dance like they're on air,
While squirrels plot a loony dare.
'Who'll climb the tree without a thud?'
All the while, the ants just shrug.

First Thoughts in Spring

A bud emerges, full of glee,
Shouting, 'Look at me, I'm free!'
The breeze snickers, playing tricks,
Pollen sneezes—oh, the kicks!

Bees hold meetings, gossip flies,
With flowers trading silly lies.
In the mix, a bumblebee—
'No one saw me—let's not spree!'

The Whispering Glade

A forest of chatter with trees that grin,
Whispers of giggles, come join in!
The mushrooms chuckle, the daisies sway,
Nature throws a party, come on, hooray!

Vines tangled like hair after a spree,
Root systems brag about who's more free.
But in the midst of all that fun,
A sleepy toad croaks, 'I'm done!'

Nature's Silent Chronicles

Raccoons wear masks, plotting their schemes,
While crickets debate the best of dreams.
The sun winks down on this funny scene,
While shadows dance, all bright and green.

With petals twirling in silly fights,
Whispers of giggles fill the nights.
A breeze that teases, just like a friend,
Says, 'This is just the beginning, not the end!'

Intrigue of New Growth

In a sprout's tiny dance, so spry,
Leaves gossip with the breeze nearby.
Roots tickle soil with a cheer,
"Hey, look at us! We have no fear!"

Beneath a sunbeam, they conspire,
To weave a tale of leafy choir.
In shades of green, they plot their play,
"Let's make the squirrels dance today!"

With whispers soft, the petals giggle,
While worms below do a little wiggle.
Telling tales of what they've seen,
"A snail just slipped—what a silly scene!"

So amid nature's circus grand,
The tiny sprouts take a stand.
With laughter fresh and breezes light,
New growth is quite the funny sight!

Time's Embrace in Nature

As leaves unfurl, they twist and shout,
"Is it time to stretch? No doubt!"
A dandelion dares to dream,
"I'll be a clock, or so it seems!"

The sun winks down, a playful tease,
While squirrels race with practiced ease.
"Oh wait, I'm late!" a twig exclaims,
As acorns drop like small, round claims.

Nature's calendar is a funny show,
Oops! A toadstool's wearing snow!
While seedlings laugh at passing birds,
"Aren't they silly with their words?"

But time moves on, with gentle grace,
Trees chuckle softly, in their place.
As shadows stretch and laughter sings,
Nature knows the joy time brings.

Tendrils of Hope

With tendrils twirling in the air,
A vine looks up with flair to spare.
"Hey, clouds! I need a lift today!"
And giggles burst in a leafy spray!

Beneath a fence, the shadows play,
In hopes they'll turn the drab to gay.
"We'll paint the world in colors bright,
And swing with joy, from day to night!"

A cheerful spritz of morning dew,
"Hey there, sun, come shine anew!"
While ants march past, on hurried feet,
"Did you hear the one about the beet?"

So bold and green, the tendrils dream,
With laughter rippling like a stream.
In every curl, there hides a jest,
In nature's arms, they feel the best!

The Forest's Gentle Gaze

In the forest where the whisper flirts,
Branches watch with leafy skirts.
"Look at the bird attempting to sing,
Like it's the next big thing!"

The trees exchange a knowing glance,
As mushrooms break into a dance.
"Let's root for them, don't be aloof,
We're all a part of this goof!"

Squirrels tumble, acorns spill,
"Did someone say it's time to chill?"
The forest giggles with gentle ease,
While flowers share their blooming tease.

With every breeze, a chuckle flows,
In nature's heart, humor grows.
A world alive with gentle plays,
In the forest's gaze, we find our ways.

A Budding Mystery

In a garden, green and bright,
A little sprout showed up one night.
With leaves so sly, it made us wonder,
What tales lie beneath its plunder.

It winks and giggles, a playful tease,
Growing tall with utmost ease.
Neighbors fret, is it a weed?
Or just a goofball planting seed?

It stretches out, it takes a bow,
The funniest plant we've seen till now.
With roots that dance and branches sway,
We're lost in laughter, come what may.

So here's to sprouts with secret schemes,
And all the foolish, funny dreams.
Who knew a bud could cause such strife?
In the garden, it's a comic life!

Quiet Murmurs of Green

In the stillness, whispers flow,
From little leaves that steal the show.
They gossip soft in leafy tones,
About the antics of gnome-like bones.

'Oh look, over there! What's that old thing?'
A snickering sound, like bells they ring.
Two ferns argue, 'I'm the taller one!'
While a dandelion chuckles—it's all for fun.

The daisies nod, as if they know,
That life is whimsical, slow and low.
The mossy floor, a trampoline,
For tiny critters, a wild scene.

So gather round, hear nature's jest,
In the shade, we can all be blessed.
With laughter shared among the green,
In this paradise, we reign supreme!

Beneath the Ferns

Underneath the ferns so grand,
Secrets thrive on mushroom land.
A beetle laughs, 'What's this fuss?'
While crickets chirp in playful truss.

A snail slides by, all slick and sly,
'You call this garden? I say goodbye!'
But his shell's too heavy, he takes a rest,
While a ladybug claims she's the best.

Butterflies giggle, beating their wings,
In this underworld, funny it brings.
A dance-off starts with roots so spry,
While ants march on by with a silly high cry.

So if you roam where shadows shade,
Remember laughter never should fade.
In the world down low, let joy be yearn,
For in every nook, there's laughter to learn!

The Language of Emerging Life

In the sprouting zone, a riddle spun,
Who knew plants could be so much fun?
With roots that tickle and leaves that tease,
Nature's humor floats on the breeze.

Little buds chatting, in whispers sweet,
Sharing stories from their leafy seat.
'Have you seen that tree with a hilarious knot?'
They laugh as they watch, their humor hot.

A bud pops out, with a fancy show,
Claiming, 'I'm ready! Look at me grow!'
While the weeds all roll in clumsy delight,
Trying to dance, but oh, what a sight!

So listen close to this verdant choir,
As plants converse and never tire.
In every laugh, in every sight,
Emerges life with pure delight!

The Unseen Growth

In a garden so bright, a sprout did arise,
With dreams of the sky and sunlit surprise.
He stretched out his leaves, oh what a sight,
But cringed at the thought of the gardener's might.

What if he's plucked, a salad in hand?
All hopes of grand heights, gone like grains of sand.
'Hey, just water me more!' he did plead with a shiver,
Hoping they'd see he's a leaf, not a sliver.

He laughed with the worms, shared jokes with the ants,
While plotting his growth, he practiced his pants—
Not made of silk, but of green leafy lace,
In hopes of impressing the ladybug race.

So while the world gazed, he sprouted with flair,
A hero unnoticed—the finest in there.
When nobody looks, that's where he will grow,
A legend of laughter, with roots far below.

Beneath the Surface

Underneath the soil, where dark secrets lay,
A party of roots was having its play.
With tulips and daisies, they danced in their space,
Sending sweet whispers to brighten the place.

One root tried to tell a rather tall joke,
But the others just chuckled, their laughter awoke.
'You're digging too deep!' laughed the onion with glee,
While the carrot just snickered, 'Just wait, you'll see!'

A busy young radish flashed bright with delight,
Claiming, "I'll grow faster, I'll reach the daylight!"
But the elder old beetroot, with wisdom in leaves,
Said, "Patience, young sprout, for the sun never grieves."

So down there they giggled, while dreaming of beams,
With plans for the garden, and a future of dreams.
While above, people worried, 'What will they become?'
Little did they know, the laughter was fun!

The Silent Awakening

In the damp of the morn, when the sun starts to peek,
A tiny green fellow arose with a squeak.
"I'm here!" he declared, with a stretch and a shake,
But the world was asleep, for goodness' sake!

A squirrel overhead was busy with nuts,
While ants lined up neatly, all dressed in their cuts.
"Look at me! I'm ready!" he shouted with cheer,
But nobody listened; oh, how he did sear!

He chirped and he chattered, crafted a crown,
With leaves made of laughter—his sunny renown.
But the breeze just replied, "You're still so quite small,
Frolic in shadows, then grow, one and all."

So he settled down, with a grin on his face,
Planning his rise, and how to win the race.
With whispers of colors, and rustles of light,
He'd soon be the star of the garden at night!

Tales of Tiny Leaves

A tale of small green, with stories to tell,
Of adventures in soil, where dreamers all dwell.
With splashes of rain and giggles from dew,
Tiny leaves spoke, with a twinkle anew.

"Last week," said a sprout, "I met a tall fern,
Who said, 'Be patient, young one, it's your turn!'
I pondered his words, while dancing in place,
'Will I grow as grand, with a swirl and a grace?'

Then one leaf chimed in, "I was near the fence,
And saw a butterfly, so huge and immense!
But I'm not afraid, for I'm clever and quick,
I'll float like the breeze, do a leaf double flick!"

So they all shared their dreams, with laughter and cheer,
In a patch that was cozy, the message was clear.
Though tiny they seemed, their spirits did soar,
For even the smallest can dream even more!

Petals of Promise

In a garden wide, in a sunny plot,
A tiny bud danced, oh what a hot spot!
Wiggling its leaves, feeling so spry,
"I'm not just a plant, I'm a pizza pie!"

The squirrels took notice, so clever and spry,
"Is that basil we smell? Oh my! Oh my!"
They toppled and tumbled, what fun to see,
Chasing the fragrance as wild as can be!

A bee buzzed around, sporting a grin,
"Hey there, little bud, let's roll with the wind!"
Together they giggled, creating a tune,
As petals turned vibrant beneath the golden moon.

With every soft sigh, they shared dreams of flight,
"Imagine us soaring, what a wondrous sight!"
So in this green patch, laughter took root,
With petals of promise, all chasing their loot.

An Unseen Journey of Growth

In the dirt so deep, where no one would peek,
A seed whispered softly, "I'm feeling quite chic!"
With nutrients galore, and sunshine for snack,
It plotted a journey, to grow and to crack!

To the left, a worm said, "Come on, take a chance!"
"I've digested my dreams, let's do a little dance!"
Together they swayed, roots shaking with glee,
"Let's reach for the sky, that's the place to be!"

But just then a snail, with a laugh so loud,
Said, "Patience, my friends! Come join my slow crowd!"
"In my world, we take our sweet time to grow,
Nibbles and giggles, that's how we flow!"

So they all held hands, this quirky little crew,
Sharing their dreams as they danced in the dew.
What a sight to behold, as they joined in a song,
An unseen journey where all could belong.

Secrets Cradled by the Wind

Two daisies conspired, heads close with a nod,
"What secrets we hold here, on this patch of sod!"
With petals a-quiver, they swayed in delight,
Whispering tales of the day and the night.

A nearby dandelion piped in with a grin,
"I can spread our secrets, let the fun begin!"
With a puff and a giggle, off flew the fluff,
"Catch us if you can, life's too short to be tough!"

The wind scooped them up, on a breath so spry,
Carrying their jokes to the vast inky sky.
Clouds chuckled along, bouncing high on each breeze,
As laughter erupted from all of the trees.

So the secrets spread wide, across fields and streams,
Connecting each blossom with hopes and with dreams.
In a world that spins fast, where joys can unwind,
It's the secrets of laughter, forever enshrined.

The Spirit of Green Underfoot

Beneath the old oaks, where the grass likes to play,
Young sprouts often giggle, skip, prance, and sway.
"Look at us, thriving, beneath this great shade,
We're the spirit of green, no plans to invade!"

A curious pebble hopped in, full of glee,
"Hey sprouts, what's the fuss? You're all after me!"
"With a little pizazz, let's start a parade!
Together we'll dance, let the games be played!"

So they twirled and they twisted, roots deep and spry,
"What a sight! What a day! Let's reach for the sky!"
Laughter erupted, tickled by sun,
As the spirit of green had truly begun.

At dusk, they all settled, dreams swirling with zest,
The pebble then chuckled, "This place is the best!"
With the moon shining down, and stars looking great,
They drifted to sleep, feeling oh so first rate.

Shadows of a Bloom

Beneath the sun, a plant did sway,
It whispered jokes throughout the day.
Its leaves would chuckle, quite absurd,
While ants would giggle, strange little herd.

The petals laughed, a colorful crew,
Tickling the breeze with a bright debut.
They told of bees that danced with glee,
And how they'd steal the nectar free.

A shadow passed, a bird on the prowl,
The plant then shivered, 'Oh, what a foul!'
Yet with a grin, it shrugged it off,
As squirrels jumped in a playful scoff.

Oh, the antics in the garden bed,
Where every sprout had laughter led.
In every bloom, a joke's embrace,
Nature's comedy reigns with grace.

The Heartbeat of the Forest

In the woods where giggles swell,
Plants spin tales, oh, can't you tell?
A fern in frills, it waves its arms,
While mushrooms chuckle with their charms.

The trees, they gossip, roots entwined,
With whispers shared, their humor defined.
A fox trots by, it trips on dew,
And laughter echoes in the view.

A beetle plans to race a snail,
The outcome's clear—a funny fail!
Yet every crawl is met with cheer,
As forest friends all gather near.

Underneath the vast green dome,
Every creature feels at home.
With laughter ringing loud and free,
It's nature's joy, wild jubilee.

A Dance of Delicate Tendrils

In the garden, the vines do twist,
With a silly dance, they can't resist.
They tickle each other, oh, what a scene,
With petals blushing, they're all quite keen.

A chicory flower wore a silly hat,
While daisies snickered, 'What's up with that?'
A pollen party with jokes galore,
Each stem a dancer, asking for more.

The morning dew drops, like tiny beads,
Sparkle with laughter, fulfilling needs.
And when the sun sets, in rosy glow,
They dream of funny shows they know.

As tendrils sway with rhythm divine,
Nature's ballet, a spirited sign.
In every bloom, a punchline grows,
A wondrous world where laughter flows.

Unfurling Dreams

Little sprouts beneath the ground,
Chuckle quietly without a sound.
'Tomorrow, we'll reach for the sky!'
They giggle together, oh my, oh my!

As morning breaks, they stretch and yawn,
With leafy jokes as a brand-new dawn.
'Who would've thought we'd grow so high?'
With giggles hidden, they wave goodbye.

A sunflower's height, it takes a chance,
Doing the limbo, giving a glance.
While clouds above begin to roam,
The plants all laugh—this earth, their home.

With each new bud, laughter's reborn,
In every leaf, a tale is worn.
So join the fun, just look around,
In this green paradise, joy is found.

Tapestry of Shadows

In a garden filled with cheer,
A tiny sprout drew near.
It wiggled and it danced,
Casting shadows, oh so pranced!

A whispering breeze that said,
"What's growing up instead?"
With roots that giggle and sway,
It promised sunshine every day!

The flowers stared in disbelief,
As branches blossomed like a thief.
"Who knew plants could have such fun?"
"Hiding laughs, they're number one!"

So take a peek in gardens bright,
Where sprouts delight, with sheer light.
For every hug from cozy soil,
There's laughter in the growing toil!

Origins of Elegance

Once a seed so small and round,
Dreamed of elegance profound.
Wiggled out from dirt so shy,
A snazzy outfit for the sky!

Put on leaves, all fresh and green,
Strutting proudly, quite the scene.
With style that could not be missed,
"I'm the trendsetter!" it hissed.

The other plants just rolled their eyes,
"Look at that sapling in disguise!
With fins so fine, it has the nerve,
To flaunt its roots, oh how they swerve!"

But elegance was just a show,
A willy-nilly way to grow.
With giggles that reached to the moon,
They each grew taller, through the tune!

The Cool Embrace of Earth

A little sprout, with roots so tight,
Said: "This earth feels just alright!"
It rocked in soil, felt the groove,
With nature's beat, it started to move!

While worms and bugs danced side by side,
It declared, "Join me! Let's take a ride!"
With a wiggle and a waddle so sweet,
Even the sunlight couldn't compete!

The rocks rolled back, giving way
To laughter shared—what a display!
With the dirt's warm hugs around,
The sprout felt joy it had found!

"Come on, friends, let's rock this place!
In our cozy little space!
With giggles bumping through the earth,
A party starts, oh what a birth!"

Legacy of Leaves

A tiny leaf with much to share,
Said, "Look at me, if you dare!"
It danced atop its twig so bold,
With secrets waiting to be told!

Around the trunk, it did a spin,
"Who needs a hat? Just look at my grin!"
The other leaves joined in the spree,
With rustling laughter and glee!

One day a breeze decided to play,
"Let's have a race, come what may!"
The leaves took flight, flying high,
Yelling, "This is our goodbye!"

Whispering tales on falling ground,
Each swirl and twirl, a joy unbound.
For every leaf that turns to gold,
Brings laughter, stories yet untold!

Whispers of the Woodland Child

In the woods where giggles grow,
A tiny tree did sway and show.
It whispered tales of squirrels bold,
While wearing acorns, bright and gold.

The mushrooms danced in puffs of green,
As leafy hats took on the scene.
The rabbits laughed, their ears all flop,
At riddles shared with every hop.

The breeze exclaimed, 'Oh what a chat!'
With secrets shared beneath the hat.
Each rustling leaf gave a wink,
As gnomes devised their plots to think.

A sapling's grin, so full of glee,
Unheard by all, yet plain to see.
In this fun grove, they all conspire,
Their laughter floats, a sweet desire.

Illuminated by Dappled Light

In beams where shadows play and leap,
The trees take vows, a secret keep.
The squirrels throw acorn confetti,
As butterflies join the dance all jetty.

A chubby robin cracks a joke,
The toadstools giggle—such a poke!
While sunbeams wink with golden cheer,
Each leaf shakes off doubt and fear.

The whispers float as flowers bloom,
Creating mischief in the room.
The hedgehogs peek with tiny grins,
For woodland wonders—let's begin!

In dappled light, they all unite,
Plotting pranks,—what a delight!
Secrets shared with cheeky flair,
In the woodland, fun fills the air.

Chronicles of the Emerging Grove

In a grove where laughter rings,
New leaves dance and jitterbug things.
A wise old oak gave them a nudge,
To tell tall tales and not to judge.

The ferns adorned in wavy hair,
Fashioned outfits to seek some flair.
The critters cheered, 'You look so fine!'
As blossoms bloomed, all intertwined.

The shadows murmured with delight,
A sneaky fox peeked left and right.
With every leap, the joy was grand,
In this forest, whimsy spanned.

The brook sang songs of bubbling fun,
While giggling twigs raced anyone.
With every bark, a story grows,
In the grove where humor flows.

The Unspoken Alliance of Flora

In a thicket where whispers start,
The flowers conspire with clever art.
They plot a prank on the passing bee,
Who dances by quite happily.

The daisies giggle, 'Watch him trip!'
As tulips prepare a secret zip.
With each flower's sway and twirl,
They concoct mischief in a whirl.

The tallest tree slid down a limb,
To eavesdrop on their chatter dim.
He chuckled low, 'That's quite the plan!'
As critters joined this joyous ran.

The roots beneath shook with delight,
In this plot felt so just right.
An alliance blooms, a sight to cheer,
For in friendship, laughter draws near.

A Young Tree's Diary

I sprouted up, small and proud,
Told the ants, "Hey, look at me!"
They laughed and danced in a crowd,
"We'll climb your trunk, just wait and see!"

Each raindrop felt like a tickle,
As worms wiggled underneath my feet.
With sunbeams, I'd always cackle,
"I'm getting taller—can't be beat!"

Squirrels chattered about my height,
"Such a tree! What leaves will grow?"
I winked and smiled, what a sight,
"I'll have the best show in the grove!"

Oh, the tales of wind and sun,
A growing tale with laughs galore.
Each twist and turn, oh what fun,
This young tree dreams of more and more!

Glimpses of Tomorrow's Canopy

When I was small, I dreamt so bold,
Of waving branches high and wide.
"Will I be strong, a sight to behold?"
As birds perched on my slender side.

The sun would shine with silly beams,
As shadows danced upon the ground.
I giggled at my leafy dreams,
While butterflies spun round and round.

What fruit will hang from my fair boughs?
Will I be tall enough for swing?
"I'll throw a party for the cows,
They'll dance and twirl; oh, what a fling!"

Each breeze could tickle, twist, and tease,
I pictured all the fun and cheer.
With laughter shared among the trees,
A canopy that all would jeer!

Whispers Beneath the Canopy

Underneath my leafy roof,
The critters gather, tales unfold.
A rabbit said, "I'm very aloof,
But your shade here is pure gold!"

A squirrel claimed he ran real fast,
He challenged me to reach the sky.
I giggled, pondered what could last,
"You'll tire out, oh fluff-brained guy!"

The winds ruffled whispers of grace,
While I stood still, a calming sight.
Each shook branch a perfect place,
For silly thoughts and pure delight.

If roots could laugh, they sure would shout,
For every giggle held within.
A banquet here with no doubt,
In laughter, all my dreams begin!

Roots of Enchantment

I dug down deep to find some cheer,
My roots reached out for a grand surprise.
Beneath the earth, I whispered, "Here!"
What wonders lie beneath the skies?

A mole popped up, all muddy and cute,
"Let's start a band beneath the ground!"
Dancing worms played every loot,
"We'd be the best! Just hear the sound!"

I chuckled at the joy we'd grow,
Each beat resonated, full of glee.
With every dig, we'd steal the show,
Roots jiving wild, down here with me.

So here's a toast, you furry friends,
In dirt we'll share our laughs, our woes.
With roots of fun that never ends,
Together in laughter, the magic grows!

A Story Written in Petals

In a garden of laughter and cheer,
Petals whisper jokes for all to hear.
"Why did the flower cross the way?
To show off its colors in bright array!"

Bees buzzing loudly, wearing shades,
Dance like they're in a fun charade.
"What do you call pollen on the run?
A sticky situation, oh, what fun!"

The daisies giggle, the tulips tease,
Telling tall tales on the warm breeze.
"Why do sunflowers always face the sun?
Because they know it's the ultimate pun!"

So gather 'round and lend an ear,
For nature's humor is always near.
With petals and laughter, life takes flight,
In this bloom-filled world, joy feels just right!

The Secret Life of Roots

Beneath the ground where few have tread,
Roots gossip loudly, it's been said.
"Did you hear about the tree on the hill?
He thinks he can dance, but he's got no skill!"

One root to another, they share a laugh,
"Hey, do you think we're on the right path?
I heard a rumor about a big old rock,
But no one will move him, he's quite the block!"

They tickle the soil and stretch out wide,
Making friends with earthworms, they take pride.
"Why do we never see the sun's bright glow?
We're underground heroes, just so you know!"

So if you think roots are quiet and meek,
Just listen closely, they've tales unique.
With giggles and wiggles, they know their worth,
Turning soil to playground, this is their earth!

Beneath the Budding Branches

Under the branches, a party abounds,
Squirrels play tag, jumping round and round.
"Why don't trees play hide and seek?
Because they can't move, what a silly streak!"

The buds whisper secrets, their voices low,
"Look at that bird, putting on a show!
He thinks he's a crooner, such a hoot,
But he's just a feathered old mula-scoot!"

The sunbeams tickle the leaves so bright,
Making shadows dance in soft morning light.
"Why are branches such great friends?
Because they always stick together till the end!"

With laughter and chatter, nature's parade,
Celebrates life, and the joy that won't fade.
From buds to blooms, it's all a delight,
Underneath branches, the mood's just right!

Soft Shadows of Growth

In the early hours, shadows stretch and play,
Little sproutlings giggle, embracing the day.
"Why do plants never get lonely at night?
Because they always have stars to hold tight!"

They stretch their leaves, reaching for jokes,
Mischief among daisies and other folks.
"What do you call a flower that tells tales?
A blooming comedian, with vibrant scales!"

In the sunlight's glow, the laughter grows,
A comedy club for the rows and rows.
"Why did the garden throw a big feast?
To feed the giggles, it's nature's least!"

So as shadows lengthen, and day turns to night,
Their whimsy continues, a jovial sight.
In the soft, dark twists, the plants still sway,
Living their humor, come what may!

The Unraveled Tangle

In the garden, sprouts do dance,
Twisting vines take their chance.
They pretend to be quite neat,
Yet trip on roots with little feet.

A snail takes charge, a mighty race,
Crawling at an unhurried pace.
It shouts, 'I'm the king, hold your cheer!'
While butterflies giggle, 'That's just too near!'

Sunshine beams, the mud does play,
In puddles where jumping jays.
A worm declares, with beaming pride,
'In this slop, we truly abide!'

The daisies whisper, 'Look and see,
What a mess, it's wild and free!'
And nature laughs, its own delight,
Tangles twisted, a comic sight.

Nature's Beneath

In the shadow of large trees,
Ants debate about the breeze.
One claims it's blowing cold,
While another shivers bold.

A beetle struts in shiny garb,
Singing tunes, a funky barb.
He thinks he's quite the sight,
While grass blades giggle, oh what a fright!

Mice in tiny suits of gray,
Hold a party just today.
With cheese as music, they do sway,
Tap dancing in the milky way!

But wise old owls just watch in glee,
Sipping tea beneath the tree.
Laughing softly, they agree,
Nature's odd, but it's the key!

Cradle of the Unseen

Beneath the ferns, the crickets play,
Creating tunes to greet the day.
They missed the memo, no one told,
About a concert meant to be bold!

With twinkling lights, a firefly flies,
In sequined suits, oh what a surprise!
He boogies bright, thinks he's a star,
While the squirrels mumble, 'He won't go far.'

Among the roots, the party's grand,
Ladybugs dance, all hand in hand.
They twirl, they spin, and oh, the fuss,
A tad of chaos, they add to the must!

But when the sun bows down with grace,
All settle in their cozy space.
'Goodnight, dear friends!' the shadows coo,
Tomorrow we'll spin a tale anew!

The Promise of Presence

In late spring, a giggle rang,
As a daisy with a lisp sang.
'Tell a joke, oh why don't you?'
But punchlines with petals just won't do!

The bees in suits, so full of chatter,
Buzzing stories that surely matter.
One bumbles close and gives a wink,
'Life's a party, don't you think?'

Caterpillars sport bow ties with flair,
Slipping slides, oh what a pair!
They wiggle and tumble, that's their style,
While moths chuckle, 'Just stay for a while!'

As shadows grow and stars appear,
The night life whispers, 'Draw near, draw near!'
Zip zap, zany, oh what a dance,
In gardens where dreams find their chance!

Growth in Stillness

In a corner of a garden bright,
A little sprout took all its might.
It stretched its leaves with all its glee,
And asked the sun to shine, you see.

A snail passed by, so slow and grand,
Said, "Hurry up, you need a plan!"
The sprout just chuckled, 'I'm in no race,
Growing is fun at my own pace.'

Raindrops giggled, tapping down,
Whispering jokes to the brown ground.
"Why did the seed feel so low?
It couldn't find where to grow, you know!"

So under skies both grey and blue,
The sprout, it danced, so bold and true.
Each day a new joke, a leafy cheer,
In stillness, it drew laughter near.

The Hidden Beauty

Once in a garden, where daisies played,
A little bulb had plans well laid.
He dreamed of colors, a grand parade,
But first, he had to escape his shade!

"Why do you frown?" asked a shy weed,
"I can't sprout flowers; I'm stuck in this creed!"
The weed just laughed and said with grace,
"Just peek out, buddy, and show your face!"

So the bulb budged, prepared for cheer,
Popped out giggling, with nothing to fear.
The neighbors gasped at the sight so bright,
"Who knew a bulb could take flight?"

So tiny he was, yet heart full of zest,
"Who knew life could be such a jest?"
Now blooming and laughing, creating a stir,
From hidden beauty, he became a blur!

Seeds of Wonder

In the soil, a party brewed,
With tiny seeds, their dreams accrued.
"Let's grow tall, like trees of fame!"
They giggled and even played a game.

A dandelion with crazy hair,
Told wild tales of flying through air.
The beans all bounced, they were so bold,
"We'll reach the sun, or so we're told!"

One seed yawned, feeling kind of slow,
"What if we just take it low?"
The others cheered, "We like your style!
Let's secretly grow for a while!"

So they burrowed deep in their cozy den,
With dreams of green, to sprout again.
A secret plot in the earth below,
Seeds of wonder, ready to show!

Underneath Pebbles

Underneath pebbles, snug and tight,
A sprightly seed dreamed of the light.
"I'll grow so tall, I'll touch the sky!"
But first, he had to say goodbye.

A worm wiggled by, with a grin so wide,
"Why waste time? Come on, let's slide!"
The seed just laughed, "I'll dig my way,
But climbing up sounds fun to play!"

As rain fell down, in splashy delight,
They danced and swirled, oh what a sight!
"Don't rush the show, let's take it slow,
Under these pebbles, we'll let it flow!"

With friendships forged in crack and crevice,
The sprout inched up, and oh, so clever!
Underneath pebbles, dreams took flight,
A funny tale of day and night.

Whispers Beneath the Soil

In hidden nooks where worms do play,
Little seeds giggle, come what may.
They toss and turn in dirt so fine,
Whispering jokes about the sunshine.

The ants march by with tiny feet,
"Oh look," they laugh, "a tasty treat!"
Tiny sprouts dream of reaching high,
While the roots grumble, "Oh my, oh my!"

A beetle shows up, thinks he's so slick,
But trips on a root, that little trick!
The daisies chuckle, waving in glee,
"Hey, watch your step, don't fall on me!"

Life underground is just grand and bold,
With laughter sprouting as stories unfold.
So next time you walk the garden path,
Remember the giggles beneath the wraths.

A Leaf's Quiet Confession

A leaf once whispered to a flower,
"I'm tired of waving for hours and hours!
What's the point of swaying in breeze,
When all I see is you and your tease?"

"Just reach for the sun, don't fret right now,
You'll sing with the wind, take a bow!"
The flower giggled, petals agleam,
"What a silly, leafy dream!"

So they plotted and poked, made mischief all day,
Turning quiet moments into a fun ballet.
They danced in the air, two friends side by side,
With laughter so bright, it couldn't be denied.

In the garden of secrets, they twirled about,
Creating a ruckus, giggling out loud.
Who knew that a leaf could have such a spark?
A little bit of joy, brightening the dark.

Dreams of the Growing Roots

Down in the dirt where the roots like to chat,
One said, "Hey, I've got this great hat!"
It's made of old grass and some shiny mud,
"Let's wear them proudly, like a big root club!"

A tiny root piped, bouncing with glee,
"I dream of the day when I'll finally see,
The world up above where the sun's always bright,
And I can make friends without losing my sight!"

Then echoes arose, as the worms joined the game,
"Don't get too lofty, don't go for fame!"
Snickers and giggles, like chains in a root,
"Stay down with us; we're all here to shoot!"

So they dreamed and they plotted, these roots filled with cheer,
"Let's keep making mischief, with laughter we'll steer!"
In the soil's warm embrace, they'd forever remain,
Crafting their dreams while dodging the rain.

Beneath the Canopy's Embrace

Under the shade where the squirrels run fast,
The leaves all chuckled, "Oh, what a blast!"
They bask in the glow of a sunbeam's light,
Making jokes about clouds drifting out of sight.

"Do you think they know, these fluffy white things,
That above their heads, we're the ones with the bling?
With jewels of dew that sparkle and shine,
While they float around, just wasting their time?"

A shadowy squirrel chimed in with a grin,
"I overheard the wind gossiping again!
He said the sun wishes it could have a peek,
But we're having too much fun; it can't take a sneak!"

So here in the woods, laughter reigns supreme,
As branches and leaves weave a joyful theme.
In the heart of the forest, beneath the green dome,
They share their delight, their playful homegrown.

The Softest Secrets

In a garden so lush, there's a whisper of green,
Where tales of the soil dance in sunlight's sheen.
Little beings giggle in their leafy attire,
While secrets exchange like notes in a choir.

A worm in a tux, what a riddle he weaves,
Tickling the roots, while the shrubbery grieves.
A snail on a stroll, thinking life is a race,
Tripping on dew drops, it's a hilarious chase.

The grasshoppers boast of their jumps and their leaps,
While ants march in line as the whole world sleeps.
Each petal a story, each bud holds a chance,
In the garden of giggles, they all do a dance.

So come take a peek at this humorous lot,
Where secrets are silly and laughter is hot.
Nature's own comedy, a whimsical play,
In the heart of the garden, mirth leads the way.

Tendrils and Time

Oh, the vines twist and twine with a twist of delight,
As they gossip with clouds in the soft morning light.
Each leaf has a tale that it wants to unfold,
Of a squirrel's wild party with acorns turned gold.

The daisies are snickering, watching the show,
As the breeze brings a joke that the daisies all know.
A lump in the mulch, with a trippy old tune,
While the grumpy old flower grumbles 'I'm immune!'

Closer you venture, the fun only thickens,
As worms tell tall tales, and the tickle-bug thickens.
With giggles of raindrops and chuckles from trees,
Every rustle's a punchline that floats on the breeze.

So here in the garden, where tendrils entwine,
Time winks at the secrets and laughs with a vine.
Life's a joke, they say, so roll with the quirk,
For every sprout here is part of the work.

The Enigma of the Earth

In a plot where the daisies wear hats with flair,
And rocks hold their breath with a quiet stare.
The crickets are masters of riddles and rhymes,
While the soil grumbles deep in its comedic crimes.

A tree with a cackle, what a sight to behold,
As it shares all the tales that the wind has told.
With roots that entwine like a chatty old crew,
Spilling the gossip of skies clear and blue.

Beetles in tuxedos parade with such pride,
While ants in their uniforms march side by side.
Each burrow a story, each twig a fine jest,
In the riddle of life, they uncover the best.

So laugh with the grasses, rejoice in the mirth,
For each little secret is part of the Earth.
In this clever design, humor blooms and prevails,
As life spins around with its funny little tales.

Beneath the Old Oak

Beneath the old oak where the shadows do play,
A comedy blossoms in a whimsical way.
With squirrels in tails that tickle the breeze,
And mushrooms in capes, they cause giggles with ease.

The roots are all rumbling, sharing fables untold,
While acorns conspire with stories bold.
Each twirling leaf whispers secrets at night,
While the owl laughs softly, making wrongs turn right.

The chipmunks play tag with the breath of the night,
As the fireflies blink their shiny delight.
A turtle's slow crawl is a joke on the move,
As it scoffs at the rush and finds its own groove.

So gather, dear friends, in this mystical shade,
Where laughter and nature have lovingly played.
For under the oak, so sturdy and grand,
The humor of life always goes hand in hand.

The Shy Embrace of Green

In a garden so cozy and bright,
A sprout tried to hide from the light.
With leaves all a-quiver, it swayed,
Shy to join in the leafy parade.

The bugs all teased, 'Come out, don't you see?
Being green isn't as scary as thee!'
But the little sprout giggled with glee,
'I'll dance with the daisies, just wait and see!'

One day, in a breeze, it felt so bold,
Wiggled its roots, as stories were told.
With a bounce and a hop, it joined in a round,
And laughter erupted from all around!

Now it sways with the flowers, quite proud,
No longer hiding, it sings out loud.
'Being small doesn't mean I can't play,
Watch me embrace this sunny day!'

The Lore of Living Wood

Old trees shared tales of the wild,
Of a sturdy branch and a giggling child.
They whispered one night, 'We have our say,
Wood sprites will dance in the moon's bright ray!'

The squirrel, quite cheeky, raised up a toast,
To nature's stories the trees loved most.
With acorns bouncing and leaves all aflutter,
They laughed so hard, they nearly fell with a shudder.

The wise old oak said, 'Don't you know?
Every twist and turn has a tale to show!'
While the willow swayed, adding, 'Join in our song,
For even the wood loves to laugh along!'

So come hear the laughter deep in the grove,
Where tales of the trees and critters rove.
With humor so light, they'll surely ensnare,
The secrets of life held in the air!

Secrets in the Sunshine

Under the sun where the daisies peek,
All the flowers whispered, oh so weak.
A dandelion said, 'I've got a trick,
I'll blow my seeds and cause quite a kick!'

The bees buzzed loud, 'We'll dance in the light!
Show us your magic, and we'll take flight!'
The dandelion chuckled, then puffed up with flair,
Sprinkling seeds everywhere, like confetti in air.

Little kids giggled, trying to catch,
The little white seeds that came with a scratch.
But with each little blow, and each giggling laugh,
The seeds floated off, like a wild, playful bath.

So if you see flowers sharing their jokes,
Know laughter is sown by the smallest folks.
And under a sky filled with joy and sun,
Life's funny secrets are just begun!

Dreams in the Loam

In a patch of rich soil, deep down in a hole,
Lived a worm who dreamed of playing a role.
'If only I'd sprout legs and could stand,
I'd prance through the garden, so grand!'

The ladybugs laughed, all shiny and bright,
'Just wiggle and squirm; that's your true flight!'
Yet the worm, with a grin, plotted grand schemes,
To leap and to soar, making big dreams!

One day, through the grass, a rabbit appeared,
Said, 'Worm, you're perfect; I'm glad that you're here!'
Together they danced, with wiggles and hops,
While the garden watched, their laughter just pops!

So remember dear friends, it's not what you lack,
Every creature's got dreams, just look at their knack.
From soil to the sky, let your passions take flight,
And laugh with the blossoms till the day turns to night!

Hidden in the Grove

In the grove where giggles grow,
A tree once danced, you wouldn't know.
It wore a hat made of leafy cheer,
Inviting all the critters near.

Squirrels wore shoes, oh what a sight!
They twirled and leaped from dusk till night.
A hedgehog DJ spun the tunes,
While possums strum on tiny loons.

Under moonbeams, shadows pranced,
Beetles whispered, "Let's take a chance!"
A firefly flared, and nearby a band,
They sang of seeds all quite unplanned.

But don't tell the oaks, they're so uptight,
They think they're wise, (but don't have the sight).
Just branches and leaves (what a dull old tale),
Meanwhile, laughter splits the gentle gale.

A Symphony of Sprouts

In the garden, sprouts hold glee,
Each tiny leaf, a note to see.
They sway to rhythms breezes hum,
While worms join in with a squiggly drum.

Carrots jive beneath the ground,
Radishes spin, all-around.
With every tickle from the rain,
The veggies laugh without a strain.

"Lettuce leads! It's a dance-off!"
Cried peas as they twirled and scoffed.
Tomatoes blushed, in red delight,
Joining in, oh what a sight!

So gather round, come one, come all,
To the serenade of the growing thrall.
Amongst the greens, the party's grand,
Where everyone joins, hand in hand.

Tread Softly Amongst the Green

In a forest where whispers talk,
A shy little tree learned to mock.
With each step, the mushrooms giggled,
As secrets and rocks all wriggled.

The owl wore glasses, quite absurd,
Reading the latest, silliest word.
The rabbits debated, 'What's a tree?,'
While dancing around, all full of glee.

"Watch your step in this jungle maze!"
Said a wise old fern with frilly ways.
"I've lost my sock! Oh where could it be?"
An acorn said, "Check near me!"

So tread lightly, dear friend, but be bright,
For cheeky trees are quite a sight.
And if you hear laughter, don't ignore,
It's just the woods, hosting the encore.

Treasures of the Forgotten

In a patch where lost toys rest,
An old shoe claimed to be the best.
It held a party for all who'd stay,
With rusty cars who danced away.

Old marbles, shiny, rolled down low,
Pretended to race, putting on a show.
A teddy bear with a curious grin,
Said, "Last time we lost, let's try again!"

A bottle cap's gotten quite round,
Echoed tales of the fun it found.
While bits of string hummed along,
United by laughter in the throng.

So if you wander past this spot,
Remember tales are worth a lot.
For treasures lie in forgotten things,
With joy and laughter that always sings.

Hope in a Little Green Shoot

In a pot, a sprout pops out,
Waving leaves, shouting, "Check me out!"
With a wiggle and a dance so spry,
It dreams of reaching up to the sky.

"I'm not just any little plant,"
Said the sprout, in a cheeky chant.
"I'll grow tall and give shade, you see,
And maybe even host a party for bees!"

A worm nearby rolls its eyes,
"Yeah, right, little friend, you're full of lies!"
But the sprout just giggled with glee,
"Wait and see, wait and see!"

In time, it stretched and stood quite proud,
With friends nearby, a merry crowd.
Its leaves danced in the soft, warm breeze,
This little plant was quite the tease!

In the Cradle of the Earth

In the soil, a giggle softly hums,
"Look at me, I'm sprouting thumbs!"
Pushing through with all its might,
Ready to bring some fun tonight.

Worms in suits throw a grand parade,
Cheering for the roots they've laid.
"You'll be the star, our leafy gem,
Don't forget us all, your little friends!"

Sunlight tickles, rain gives a splash,
"I'm growing up, faster than a flash!"
The daisies laugh, but the sprout just beams,
"Catch me if you can, I'm chasing dreams!"

In the cradle of all that's green,
Funny things happen, if you know what I mean.
Nature's laughter fills the air,
With roots like jokes that dance everywhere!

The First Breath of Nature

A bud woke up with a yawning cheer,
"Finally, I'm out of here!"
It stretched its leaves, what a funny sight,
Whispering secrets to the morning light.

"Who knew this world would be so grand?"
Said the bud, as it wobbled, not quite planned.
"I might tip over, but that's okay,
I'll just roll around, ready to play!"

The bees tickled it with tiny wings,
"We're off to a garden party; come join our flings!"
But the bud just giggled, flipped its hair,
"I may be small, but I'll get there!"

Taking the plunge, into the sun,
Breathing deep, oh what fun!
With nature's laughter, a song so sweet,
The first breath comes, can't feel my feet!

Gentle Roots and Skyward Dreams

Beneath the earth, the roots hold tight,
Whispering secrets through the night.
"We're the feet, oh can't you see?
Our dreams are growing, just like a tree!"

A leaf popped up, all bright and bold,
"Hey, down there, come hear the story told!"
"Of sunlit days and raindrop laughs,
Join us in our leafy crafts!"

Matters of growth, oh what a chase,
Roots find friends in every place.
"Upward and onward, let's climb the beam,
We're here to make the world a meme!"

In playful jests, they stretch and sway,
Chasing giggles through every day.
Gentle roots and dreams that beam,
Life's a garden, or so it seems!

Secrets in the Shade

Under the leaves, the whispers play,
Tiny secrets dance and sway.
A squirrel giggles, a bird just sighs,
Nature's jokes are no disguise.

Who knew that roots could tell a tale?
Of wobbly worms and a breezy gale.
The sunbeam chuckles, the grass is keen,
All while I sip my dandelion tea.

A flower blushes, shy and bold,
With petals wrapped in stories untold.
The breezes tickle, the shadows grin,
While I wonder what mischief could begin!

Leaves rustle softly, what a delight,
A round of giggles in the soft twilight.
Nature's laughter fills the glade,
With every leaf, a joke is made.

The Language of Young Bark

In the talking woods, a bark brigade,
Chattering branches, a raucous parade.
The trees have tales of grand old days,
In knotty voices, they sing and play.

A young birch leans in, 'What's the scoop?'
As the oak replies with a mighty whoop.
Pine cones tumble, laughter spills,
In every creak, the woodland thrills!

The saplings gossip, hear their jokes,
Twisting and turning, they poke fun at folks.
With every rustle, the cheer grows strong,
'Come join our dance, come sing along!'

The bark, it snickers, 'I'm not just wood!'
'There's wisdom here, misunderstood!'
In nature's choir, where fun ignites,
We learn from trees on starry nights.

Tender Souls in Nature

In the forest's heart, the soft rain drips,
Where flowers gossip and starlings flip.
A ladybug chuckles on a green leaf throne,
While a snail shares stories, never alone.

Beneath the ferns, a ticklish breeze,
Has butterflies giggling among the trees.
Every droplet holds a chuckling cheer,
As they dance on petals, what a sight here!

A lady's mantle whispers secrets so sweet,
As ants march along, shuffling their feet.
'Are we late?' they fret, in a rush to behold,
The grand dance of nature, a tale to be told.

Soft shadows play with the light of day,
While the daisies hum softly, in their own way.
In this tapestry where laughter unfolds,
Even the tiniest tenders have stories bold!

Echoes of Green Innocence

In the grove where silliness reigns supreme,
The crickets debate the best ice cream.
While hedgehogs hug the trees with flair,
Sipping on nectar from flowers rare.

The whispers between the daffodils sing,
'What's behind that big old swing?'
A shy bluejay fluffs its feathery coat,
As the fireflies tease to make them float.

Toadstools gather for a parties' start,
With hopscotch lines and a leafy chart.
As the mushrooms chuckle underfoot,
A giggly breeze brings mischief to boot!

Nature's echo, a playful refrain,
Filled with the joy of sunshine and rain.
In this whimsical land where laughter grows,
Every heart opens, and wonder flows.

Beneath the Surface

Underneath the soil's crust,
Worms are hosting dance parties,
Roots are practicing their spins,
While moles tell wild, funny stories.

Tiny seeds are making plans,
Plotting how to reach the sky,
They giggle at their lofty dreams,
While ants strut by, oh so spry.

When rain drops start to fall in glee,
They're jumping like they've lost their shoes,
Pitter-patter, listen close,
The ground's a stage for silly blues.

What a surprise when sprigs arise,
With laughter written on each leaf,
Nature's jesters, lively pranks,
In whispers, bring us sweet relief.

Life Awakens

Awakening with morning light,
A snail races at snail's pace,
While frogs croak their morning tunes,
Inviting all to join the race.

The flowers blush in frilly gowns,
Dancing in their colors bright,
Bees buzzing by like comic stars,
In search of nectar, quite the sight.

Chirping birds in rhythmic jokes,
Raccoons chuckle in the trees,
A squirrel sets up acorn stands,
Preparing for nutty festivities.

As day breaks with a joyful cheer,
The world is ripe for laughter's spark,
In nature's play, we find our peace,
Oh, springtime's fun is in full mark.

A Heartbeat of Leaves

Leaves are whispering secrets low,
Tickling branches in the breeze,
They'd giggle, if they had a voice,
Joking about the bumblebees.

Each rustle tells a funny tale,
Of birds that tried their best to fly,
But landed with a thump and thud,
In the branches, not quite shy.

The sun peeks through in streaky beams,
To spot the antics of the day,
A caterpillar slips and slides,
In spirals, practicing ballet.

Oh, how nature plays its cards,
With laughter woven in the green,
A heartbeat in these leafy bounds,
With rhythm, truest joy is seen.

Nature's Nursery Rhyme

In a clearing, merry sounds,
Nature sings in playful rhyme,
Squirrels leap with silly steps,
Chasing shadows on a dime.

The daisies giggle, having fun,
With petals waving to the sun,
Each bee takes a turn to dance,
A buzz, a twirl, then on the run.

Worms in soil envision grand balls,
With party hats made out of leaves,
While butterflies crack silly jokes,
At flowers wearing perfume thieves.

The brook gurgles its sweet refrain,
Of ducks in rafts, oh what a sight,
Nature's nursery rhyme delights,
With laughter echoing in the light.

The Mysteries of Spring's Hands

Spring's hands mold the earth with care,
Tickling buds to wake and grow,
With every pat and tender touch,
A giggle hides in every row.

The crocuses push through the chill,
With grins that bloom in yellow,
While centipedes roll in the grass,
Creating paths, oh what a fellow!

The rain drops down like kids on swings,
Splashing puddles with delight,
While clouds tease with their fluffy shapes,
Molding laughter, pure and bright.

In every corner of the park,
A funny scene unveiled unfolds,
Nature's secrets, silly fun,
In spring's embrace, the world beholds.

www.ingramcontent.com/pod-product-compliance
Lightning Source LLC
Chambersburg PA
CBHW051658160426
43209CB00004B/939